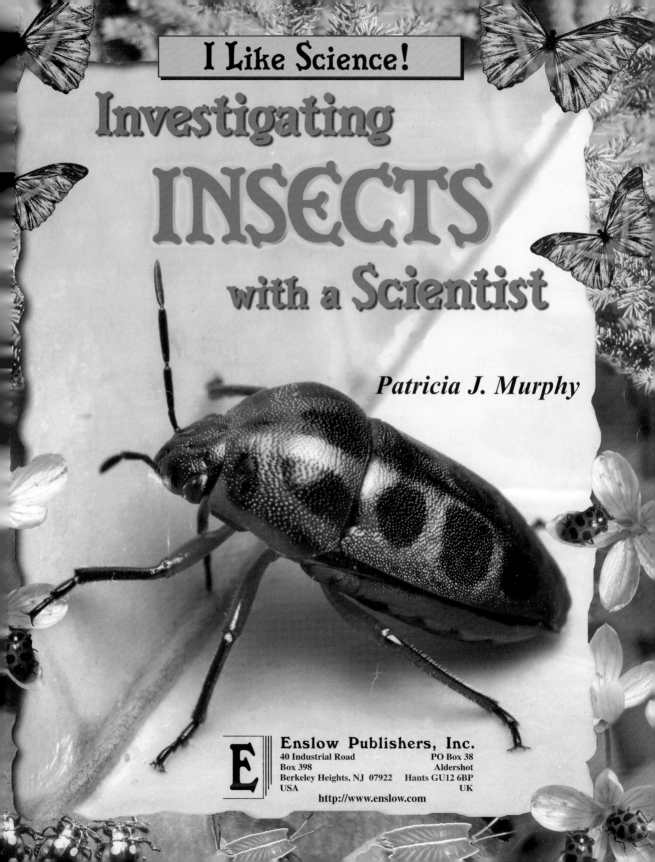

I Like Science!

Investigating
INSECTS
with a Scientist

Patricia J. Murphy

E
Enslow Publishers, Inc.
40 Industrial Road   PO Box 38
Box 398   Aldershot
Berkeley Heights, NJ 07922 Hants GU12 6BP
USA   UK
http://www.enslow.com

Contents

Words to Know

antennae (an TEN ee)—The long feelers on the head of an insect.

experiment (ek SPER ih ment)—A test done by scientists.

microscope (MYE kruh skohp)—An instrument that makes small objects look bigger.

pollen (PAH lun)—The yellow powder in a flower. Pollen helps plants make seeds.

Look. Listen.
Crawl on the ground.
Insects are everywhere!

Insects make up most of the animals
on Earth. And, that is a *good* thing.
We need them.

3

What is an insect?

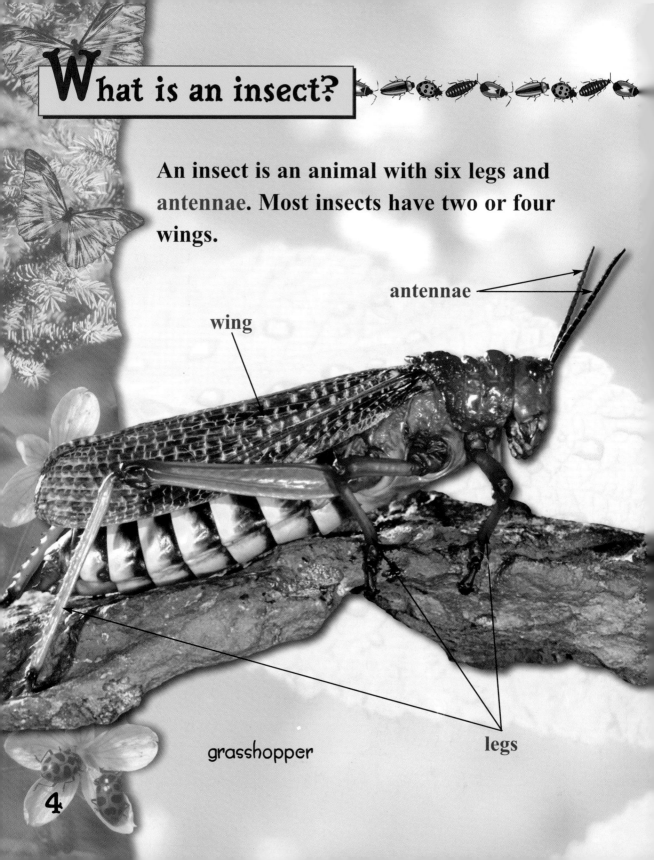

An insect is an animal with six legs and antennae. Most insects have two or four wings.

antennae

wing

legs

grasshopper

4

Flies, grasshoppers, and ants are insects.
So are beetles, mosquitoes, and butterflies.

Most insects hatch from eggs.

Why do we need insects?

Some insects spread **pollen** from flower to flower. This helps plants make seeds and fruit. Some seeds and fruit are eaten by people and other animals. Other seeds grow into new plants.

Many insects are food for other animals such as frogs, fish, lizards, and birds. In some parts of the world, even people eat insects!

Meet Insect Scientist May Berenbaum.

Scientist May studies insects. She does experiments to learn more about them.

She looks at how insects and plants live together.
She writes books about insects, too.

Where do insect scientists work?

Insect scientists follow insects around the world. Some scientists work outdoors. They travel to rain forests, deserts, and cornfields.

Other insect scientists work indoors. They work in labs, offices, museums, or classrooms.

How do scientists collect insects?

Scientists may hang from tall trees or crawl on their stomachs to find insects. They use nets or traps to catch insects.

Next, they bring the insects into a lab. Then the scientists can study the insects up close.

What tools do scientists use to study insects?

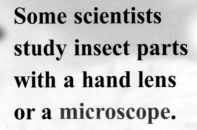

Some scientists study insect parts with a hand lens or a microscope.

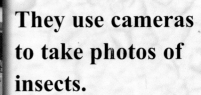

They use cameras to take photos of insects.

This scientist is using a microscope that can take pictures.

mosquito
antennae

eye

These photos
were taken
with a special
microscope.

butterfly wing scales

Scientists ask questions. They take
measurements. They write about what
they see. They put the new facts into
computers and on the Internet. This lets
scientists share the new facts.

15

How do scientists keep track of insects?

Many scientists sort insects into different groups. Insects that look and act the same are put in the same group.

16

These groups help scientists keep track of the world's one million types of insects. Scientists believe there may be 35 million more!

Why does Scientist May study insects?

Scientist May studies insects to learn their secrets. Which plants do they like to eat? How can farmers stop insects from eating their plants? Scientist May looks for answers.

parsnip plant

webworm

Webworms are caterpillars that turn into moths. They eat parsnip plants.

18

When Scientist May was young, she was afraid of insects. Today, she cannot imagine studying anything else. She says, "With so many insects, I'll never get bored."

What kinds of insects are around you?

You will need:
- ✔ an adult
- ✔ hand lens
- ✔ clear jar with screw-on lid (Ask an adult to put air holes in the lid.)
- ✔ butterfly net
- ✔ notebook
- ✔ pencil

Safety tip: Some people are allergic to insect bites and stings. Beware of all biting and stinging insects.

1. Go outdoors with an adult. Look for insects on flowers, bushes, and trees.

2. Study them under a hand lens. Draw sketches and take notes. Write down how they move and what they eat.

3. Catch some insects with a net. Put them in a small jar. Look at your insects. Ask questions like:

What kind of insects are they?
What are their colors or shapes?
How do they act and move?
Where did you find them?
Are different insects on different plants?

4. Let your insects go.

5. Read books about your insects. Write reports, poems, or stories about them. Put your notes, sketches, and writings in a notebook.

Learn More

Books

Holland, Gay W. *Look Closer: An Introduction to Bug-Watching*. Brookfield, Conn.: Millbrook Press, 2003.

Jackson, Donna M. *The Bug Scientists*. Boston: Houghton Mifflin, 2002.

Penner, Lucille Recht. *Monster Bugs*. New York: Random House, 2003.

Pike, Katy. *Insects*. Philadelphia: Chelsea House Publishers, 2003.

Reinhart, Matthew. *Young Naturalist's Handbook: Insect-lo-pedia*. New York: Hyperion Books for Children, 2003.

Solway, Andrew. *Classifying Insects*. Chicago: Heinemann Library, 2003.

Stewart, Melissa. *Maggots, Grubs, and More: The Secret Lives of Young Insects*. Brookfield, Conn.: Millbrook Press, 2003.

Web Sites

© Earthlife Web Productions. *Welcome to the Wonderful World of Insects.*
<http://www.earthlife.net/insects/six.html>

Encyclopedia Smithsonian. *Entomology.*
<http://www.si.edu/resource/faq/nmnh/buginfo/start.htm>

The Science Spot Kid Zone. *World of Insects.*
<http://www.sciencespot.net/Pages/kdzinsect.html>

Index

To my little insect lovers: Bailey, Erik, and Olivia

Series Literacy Consultant:
Allan A. De Fina, Ph.D.
Past President of the New Jersey Reading Association
Professor, Department of Literacy Education
New Jersey City University

Science Consultant:
May R. Berenbaum, Ph.D.
Head, Entomology Department
University of Illinois

Note to Teachers and Parents: The **I Like Science!** series supports the National Science Education Standards for K–4 science, including content standards "Science as a human endeavor" and "Science as inquiry." The Words to Know section introduces subject-specific vocabulary, including pronunciation and definitions. Early readers may require help with these new words.

Library of Congress Cataloging-in-Publication Data

Murphy, Patricia J., 1963–
    Investigating insects with a scientist / Patricia J. Murphy.
        p. cm. — (I like science!)
    Includes bibliographical references (p.   ).
    ISBN 0-7660-2270-6 (hardcover)
    1. Insects—Juvenile literature. 2. Entomologists—Juvenile literature. [1. Insects. 2. Entomologists. 3. Occupations.] I. Title. II. Series.
    QL467.2.M885 2004
    595.7—dc22
                            2003026959

Printed in the United States of America

10 9 8 7 6 5 4 3 2 1

Photo Credits: ©2002–2004 ArtToday, Inc., pp. 1, 3, 4, 5, 9, 19; © Bill Beatty/Visuals Unlimited, p. 6; Copyright Dennis Kunkel Microscopy, Inc., p. 15; © 2004 Gary Braasch, pp. 10, 11, 12, 13 (bottom), 14 (top right), 16, 17; © Gary Meszaros/Visuals Unlimited, p. 7; John T. Longino, p. 13 (top); Lawrence Migdale/Photo Researchers, Inc., p. 14 (bottom left); Photo by Richard Leskosky, p. 8; Photo by Norman Hagan, 2002, p. 18.

Cover Photo: ©2002–2004 ArtToday, Inc.